Witch Wife

Witch Wife

Poems

Kiki Petrosino

Sarabande Books
Louisville, KY | Brooklyn, NY

Library of Congress Cataloging-in-Publication Data

Names: Petrosino, Kiki, 1979- author.
Title: Witch wife : poems / by Kiki Petrosino.
Description: First edition. | Louisville, KY : Sarabande Books, 2017. |
Includes bibliographical references and index.
Identifiers: LCCN 2017002605 (print) | LCCN 2017002874 (ebook) | ISBN
9781946448033 (hardcover : acid-free paper) | ISBN 9781946448040 (ebook)
Classification: LCC PS3616.E868 A6 2017 (print) | LCC PS3616.E868 (ebook) |
DDC 811/.6--dc23
LC record available at https://lccn.loc.gov/2017002605

Interior and exterior design by Kristen Radtke.

Manufactured in Canada.
This book is printed on acid-free paper.
Sarabande Books is a nonprofit literary organization.

This project is supported in part by an award from the National Endowment for the Arts. The Kentucky
Arts Council, the state arts agency, supports Sarabande Books with state tax dollars and federal funding
from the National Endowment for the Arts.

One

Two

In memory of my grandmothers

Cleopatra Beverly
Michelina Petrosino

forza e dolcezza

One

Self-Portrait

Little gal, who knit thee?
      Dost thou know who knit thee?
Gave thee milk & bid thee beg
Slid a purse between your legs
Stuffed thy brain with blooms of blight:
algae, wool. You're lichen-white.
Gave to thee such vicious lungs
for breathing glitter past your wrongs—

      Little gal, I'll tell thee
      Little gal, I'll tell thee!
I, who cut your palms with glass
& poured in poison *tasse* by *tasse*
I am nimble. I am young.
I peeled you with a pair of tongs.
I laughed when no one loved you back
& raked the mist to scarf your flesh.
We come together in the dirt.
I a rake & thou a twig;
      All day we watch the long pig dig.
      All day we watch the long pig dig.

Young

After Anne Sexton

A thousand pilot lights ago
when I'm a teenager half-gone to flab
in a low ranch house crammed
with ribboned handicrafts in January
I go pulling all the false candy canes
from the stale mulch out front
clown-sun blinking whitely over me
my bedroom window an ear
painted shut to keep the calliope of dreams
from sounding. Nearby, the Douglas Fir
thickens over older strings of lights, the chipped
blue bulbs & the gold, each wrapped in peeling floss
& held by keloids to the scruff
of an unloved trunk. Probably a million tiny
ice crystals drift on their rainbow way
while the feverish branches chafe & flake
& I, in my runny custard body
with its buried corkscrew of hate
tell the tree my story-songs
& think God can really hear
above the cold & the snapping plastic canes
boots, belly, my dreams, what's wrong.

New South

am born
light girl, light girl
each step blessed but slant
born in procession
already my mother, her mother
the same her mother, then
her mother the same
marching by night
under southern pines
or a dream of pines
on the night road
my feet grown strange
my neck turning back
over the dream of land
we left or never left
land of trouble where
I'm always marching
my hair cropped close
my mothers beside me
in robes & crowns so
I go back, go forth
light girl, light girl
crammed with light
& when my mothers say
don't you tell them about us

13

don't you ever tell
I look down hard
at my hands
white webs opening
somehow
strange to
myself

This Is How We Feed the Animals

First, we call them: *Blood-Beasts. Double They.*
We sense them shining in our net of nerves.
Countless. Pelted. Their mint-smoke smell, closer
than we thought. This is how we track them
with our bone dice, how we dig them a hole
with the knives of our teeth. Will they fall in?
We wait. But when we look, nothing has fallen.
We throw some fresh hay into the hole. We lie
in the sun, considering names. We think
they have names. We think they secrete a liquor
from their tongues which is a cure. Just once
we kissed them: a season of air. But they
wouldn't stay, or drink from our hands. Now
they come in the dark to hang their muzzles
over our fence lines. We seem to feel their breath
on our backs at night. This is how it is for us
when the egg of sleep will not break:
Grief-Marked. Heart-Lost.

Contagion

I wake up in my body & it's worse
than a war zone. My smoke-cloud of blood
my hair grenade *tick tick boom*. It's worse than
a war zone when I cruise past your brunch. Just
to get bread. Just ordering juice. I open my mouth
& the War rolls out, dense as a foghorn. I can't
keep from squeezing my skull. I keep time-traveling
back to the noon of my birth. Worse than a war zone
that Sunday, that night, when I wept in the War
of myself. That's the first war I knew. It was worse
than a war.

Maria

She'd appear in the break before sleep.
Her face a glass zero. Her dark buzzing.
I was twelve. I sweated & begged

to live. Back then, I believed she could
spike me with faith, a silverweed stolon—
she'd appear in the break before sleep

pronouncing my name in her language
of radial burn. *Name, name, name, name.*
I was twelve. I sweated & begged

in the dark. My sins hummed between us
a ravel of birds, a lightning smell.
She'd appear in the break before sleep

& drift close. As if my face
were hitched to a track which pulled her.
But I was twelve. I sweated & begged

until she dissolved: empty oval of air.
Now I can't think what I wished for instead.
How I sweated & begged in the break before sleep.
I was twelve. I was twelve. I was twelve.

Elegy

You died in the pith of August. You left us.
In rageful choke, in dust: you left us.

On your coffin lid: *Going Home*. A bluebird there.
Plastic ribbons dripping down. You left us

in a welter of bells & holy water. The Word
of the Lord glazed shut the day. You left us

to our sweat & our complaints, to our swollen wood-
pulp tongues. Of course we U-turned, left

the wrong way home. No birds
glimmered through the balding pines. You left us

to bleat & blister ourselves out, but my words
hung, paint-thick in my chest. Nothing you left us

made sense. Your college of clay cardinals, each bird
a tiny fist of time. Is that what's left of us

down here? Absent engine, steel-hulled bird
I was laughing over coffee when you left us

for the edge of space. You must've felt a sword
of light draw down your spine, & then—you left us

honeycombed, here. No words for the slur
of days that have wept through the world since you left us.

& though I'm middle-named for you (*Michelle*, a word
for the angel who salts the earth you left us

digging in) my first name knits a tighter cord:
Courteney, dark dweller. I wait where you left us.

Whole 30

After a winter of gluttony & grief
I'm back on plan for good this time.
I've ballooned to a specific kind of ugly

the kind you hope to hide
with body spray. But it gets worse
after a winter of gluttony & grief.

I've shown up for meatballs. For lemons
whipped to weeping. Now I land my balloon
for the specific kind of ugly

salad oil is. Happy date night, darling.
Happy coconut water + nutritional yeast.
After this winter of gluttony & grief

spring comes, stabbing her hard stem
of anger in the throat. Even garlic scapes
are flat balloons, their ugliness specific

as my penmanship: green tubes of spice
& hate. My body speaks the ugly testament
that took all winter. It says: *Gluttony & grief*
balloon, darling. Only kindness is specific.

Thigh Gap

It's true: I have it
though I hardly approve
of anything it does.

Supposed bend of light
or smudge where two odd
angles cross. I hardly see—

can hardly do a thing
with it. White zone of
no flesh pressing

into no. So low, I can't
scale or measure it. I used
to think: *OK! A clean sharp place*

to keep. Or: *I'll grow*
a thing! to keep, for me! But
no. It's just a ward

to mark & mount, a loop
I lope around with, so
I count

myself a realm
of realms. I vote & vote.
Turns out, we agree

with everything we
do, almost. We sweep
the precincts

of ourselves: the rooms
between each rib
& under them

till we reach the fat
red condo where
our blood leans in.

We live here now. Half
heart, half townhouse.
Come on down.

Turn on that sweet TV.
Our *mise en place*, our rugs
& nooks: we're full

of stuff. We paint
the furniture we couldn't
live without. It's true

at last: we have it all
though we hardly know
what any of it does.

First Girdle

For this glob of a girl who feeds like a grub. For her teeming belly-apron. For her frowning navel, sunk like a moon in the night-night lake. For the soft eggs of flab that hatch in her. For marbled thighs & indigo veins, her mattress flank. For a form of firmness, plastic lace tacked down with hidden rivets. For the crisscrossed orbitals of redness at her waist, the pinching tugs she sneaks to force the hems of her culottes down. Poor poreless receptacle for Presidential-fitness-test-sweat, poor pudding poured into too few pans. They haven't made the polymer that may forgive her, yet. No pastel mesh exists to hold the semisweet chips melting in her mitts, nor the ingots of cold butter she filches from the fridge. What would you give to shunt her starfish hands & aphid appetite? Does anybody have a knife?

Voice Lesson

Hello, dumb vain Bird of Paradise.
Time to shred your lungs' silk kerchief.
You can't be pretty mouth & sing.

Want some orange *pip pip pip*s?
Ain't you lonesome on your little swing?
You dumb vain Bird of Paradise.

I see you doling seeds & ants to nobody.
What a drag. You ain't made for onliness.
You can't be pretty mouth & sing!

All alone, all alone, all alone, all alone—
Make your *O* like an egg. Like an egg, see:
Hell-*O*. You dumb vain Bird of Paradise.

Don't swallow them stones. They dead
like you might be awful soon, if you please.
You can't be pretty mouth & sing.

Just how long will you peck around here
when you ought to belt & caw? *Halloo.*
Halloo, you dumb vain Bird of Paradise.
You can't be pretty mouth & sing.

Little Gals

They come at night
on membranous
wings. I'm a soft deer
browsing the woods
with strands of willow
in my pelt.

When they lean in
to call me out
I shiver & shine
in my thicket
of one.

Do they know
about the botch
in my belly? I think
it's a gel
where the white light
rots.

One says *You know
it's past time you bred*
& opens her mouth
full of egg teeth.

You must have
some kind of hatch for it
says another
Or hole says the third
clicking.

All three hang
in the night air
identical silk faces
identical jaw wires
wanting to scoop me
into their high
humming.

I gallop deep
in shade
past grease-marked trees
to the lake
where March mud dashes
up my burning
26   legs.

But soon
I feel them again
at my belly
spinning
their round nymphal
selves, pressing
their hundred
eyes.

There is
a red delight
in the heat & snap
of their pincers.
They've made themselves
so much finer this time
new mouthparts
new bodies burrowing
all through my undercoat
where I let them dig down
into the dim
places.

Sermon

Who shall change my vile body into a glorious body
when I know there's glory at the end of my prayer?
Who shall change my vile body into a glorious body?

A lioness subdues all things to herself.
Yes, even a lioness subdues all things to herself.
Who shall change my vile body into a glorious body?

When I talk to the lioness, sometimes she answers.
When I talk my dragging talk, this is how she answers:
Your vile body shall change into a glorious body.

I've planted my claws in the lioness nation.
With my claws in the dirt, I've pledged a whole nation.
But who shall change my vile body into a glorious body?

The Lord makes a lioness. She multiplies in gold.
The Lord makes a wild lioness. Let her multiply in gold.
But how shall my vile body change into a glorious body?

O Lord, if my real life is the lioness hunting—
if she'll crown me with thunder when I get to her country—
only then shall I come into glory, Lord
when I drown when I drown when I drown when I drown.

Two

Pastoral

Where did it start? In a city of gardens & muck.
When I held someone close, in watery light.
We drank & I bled all the way home.

Red-orange light on my legs. *Oh, wow—*
that blink-blink of bright, that flip of the pulse.
Where did it start? In the garden, the muck

where insects jumped in starry arcs. My body
took shape, then. A greenhouse I entered alone.
We drank & I bled all the way home.

I wore so many clothes. Cotton, cotton, wool.
I burned in my skin like a stone. How exactly?
Where did it start? There, in the muck

no one saw how we blazed into poppies.
Light raked through our bellies like combs.
We drank & I bled all the way home.

Now, I blister up from bed. My love
is a silver cry in the light. *O animal life—*
in a city of gardens & muck, you can start

to itch. You jostle & fight, scrambling
for years up the hill of your life. You ask
Where does anything start? In muck. In a garden.
You drink the drinks & bleed. You're foam.

Nocturne

After Mark Strand

I fill my plate with rain. I fill my belly.
I fill a T-shirt with shells & count them on the floor.
At night, I drink juice from a moon-colored mug.
I feed the lamp & wrap my hair in a scarf.

What good am I doing? The ocean whines from bed.
I take my pills. I bury watermelon seeds.
The pills & the seeds move past each other in the dark.
Who blesses them?

When I slither up from sleep,
my regrets are shreds of pulp in my mouth.
It's true that I love & that I do not love.
I fill myself with my regrets & begin to speak.

Twenty-One

Journal, mixtape, leather coat.
Silk scarf painted with caducei.
Lunapark, broom flowers, ferryboat.
Ticket stub: Autobus 25.

Birthstone anklet, white Peugeot.
Journal, mixtape, leather coat.
Perseid shower, bear paw charm.
Lunapark, broom flowers, ferryboat.

Thumb ring, tank top, lucky coin.
Birthstone anklet, white Peugeot.
Pastasciutta, freckled arms.
Perseid shower, bear paw charm.

Campfire, windsurf, sudden wine.
Thumb ring, tank top, lucky coin.
Olive orchard, sunflower farm.
Pastasciutta, freckled arms.

Yogurt with apricots. Coca-Lite.
Campfire, sudden wine, windsurf.
Olive orchard, sunflower farm.
Laundry, terrace, Sting concert.

Feather earrings, volcano hike.
Yogurt, apricots, Coca-Lite.
Green-yellow sunset. Fever sleep.
Terrace. Laundry. Sting. Sting.

Study Abroad

No chance you're pregnant the English doctor asked. *No chance* you repeated slowly, then added *No chance.* That was the summer all Tuscan girls wore green cargo pants & orange camisoles. It looked one way, shopping at Esselunga, & another in the piazza with your tumbler full of strawberry liqueur & the first blue stars catapulting over the Arno. The doctor resembled a townhouse, his hair peaked narrowly in the middle. Your fingers, in their closed fists, made a subtle heat exclusive to your experience. You took the green-yellow pills, thinly coated with sweetness & punched into a paper card. Weeks later, you let your companion take you into the woods by the beach. In his family's summer house, you broke some old chairs to feed the fire, & the stem of your body unspooled in every room. Then you slipped your long feet into the green sandals you hadn't realized were python leather until the scales had already kinked & dulled. You will never have another pair like that. Not real python.

Europe

Every night, I go back to your house
behind the abandoned *caserma*, where once
I wept in my clothes on the street.

Your same window with its rolling blinds.
Same diesel smell. Same birds on the roof.
Every night, I go back to your house.

I almost dissolved when you sank
your verbs in white ink: imperfect, subjunctive.
I wept in my clothes on the street

where olive trees turned their foil palms.
It was summer. I stood in my smithereens.
Every night, I go back to your house

climbing your melted marble steps. My age
is a seed-pearl under my tongue. Was I wrong
to weep in my clothes on the street?

Your lamps are still. Your mother is home.
I'll never be so lonely again, or young enough
to weep in my clothes on the street.
Every night, I go back to your house.

Why Don't You Wear a Black Crepe Glove Embroidered in Gold, Like the Hand That Bore a Falcon?

You are describing how the transparent oval of my face seems to hang before you in the seconds before sleep. I peel off my gloves to eat from your paper cone of burning chestnuts even though they taste like bugs to me. You buy the chestnuts because you want me to enjoy this trip but then never to come back, not to your bedroom where I left my footprint in lotion on the hardwood, not to sit with you before your mother's scant bowls of *pastina in brodo*. We pass the newsstand next to the bakery next to the bus stop by the restaurant that used to be an orphanage. You're still talking about my phantom face, about the white light which, you say, surges into a beautiful tree-shape on top of my head. The clarity of this light magnetized your soul, or perhaps your soul already contained the exact spinning glob of sweetness that matched my own. It would be wrong to say precisely, it would be wrong to remember in any particular fashion. Our futures float by in their clear bulbs of breath, & I tell you the story again.

Break-Up-A-Thalamion

You don't share
your scones with me anymore
even though you said
I'd have all your *buon*
sostegno per sempre.

I don't care
for your bakery smug.
I'm crying you out.
My tears are cold cubes
springing off my face
like cartoons.

Hey.
You're a punch
in the head. Nobody
will tell you so
but me.

Let Me Tell You People Something

The women in my country, they are going into the yard with pots & spoons to bang at crows. Always, this. Because crows will eat every fruit from the trees, & then? Nothing left. So the women bang, they yell in a big voice every morning. But crow is not afraid of woman, it will come back tomorrow. Crow is like, you bring pot & spoon? I do not care. You know, *do not care*? Tomorrow, maybe, you leave this city. You take just one small box or one small case, fly to another house, put your box on the floor & ask: this box, who is it? Who lives in my house? You are forgetting all the time. I have seen you, wearing the name of your city on the T-shirts. Every name more huge, lying across the chest like a creature. Always, you complain in your small clothes. You complain when the rain is not stopping, but also: no rain. This complaining you do? Is just the ghost of the house you leave for another house. You don't remember. But. In my country, we take the young asparagus in March when it walks on the hills. Asparagus is like the persons we have loved, standing in the house of our parents. I am living here for many years now, but I do not forget my mother in the yard. My sister with her spoon. I do not weep in your way of ghosts. That's all.

Political Poem

The country is not what it was. I miss the arc of
green fireworks in spring & the moral
bellies of lake trout rolled in flour. This universe is
so dry, star-sharp. Each day, my arms grow long but
never reach the freedom shore. The line of it bends
like a fern in rain. Birds chatter towards justice

towards justice towards justice towards justice—
Their beaks click together like dolls. I study the arc of
my own slithering chin as it bends
along the waterway of my phone. The moral
is a glass canoe lodged in a long but
finite block of news. I say: *This universe is*

not worth my heard-earned glitter. This universe is
not what I dreamed. Wings careen in the blue, towards justice
but I watch from the dirt, my feet burning. I long, but
I can't measure my longing, can't trace the arc of
my tears as they depart from my head. Now the moral
autobus kneels like a camel at the curb. It bends

& I climb into the sinking dark. I climb. It bends.
This forced union is not what I've loved. What's a universe?
A tingle up my leg. The stars. Once, I dreamed a moral
constellation of strawberry seeds, arranged towards justice.

But I don't know how to read stars, the arc of
federal dust that governs me. My body is long, but

not quite free. I go along, I get along, but
I'm not quite free. My sweet, harmless body, it bends
so you can't identify my color, just the arc of
my spine, which could be anyone's, in the cool universes
of love. So let my body move towards justice
& away from countries. Let it curl up like the moral

fortune still inside the cookie, the moral
border dissolving in cold milk. Won't be long.
Will everything we know collapse towards justice?
Bodies, berries, beaks, barns—will all of it bend
& wash under the moon? It feels like this universe is
someone else's calculus, the arc of

a moonbeam in the moral firmament. It bends
& the light is long, but dimming. Such universes.
Here, I draw the arc of two words: *just is.*

Afterlife

My exes shall rise up from their Mazdas
& adorn themselves in denim.

I'll take their hands & we'll wander
among the silver asparagus.

Though all are present, it seems to each
that I'm walking with him only.

One brings me five white roses again
petals curling in soft paper.

Another comes with a mixtape & drawings:
heart, suitcase, shape of his country.

We'll sit at the stone table & eat
from the same jar of strawberries & mint.

Each will tell about his wife. The golden hikes
they take after lunch with their dogs.

I'll show them my books & the healed mark
over my ribcage.

We'll enter the cottage where our babies sleep
forever in their small beds.

I'll hum to them in many voices until just
one brightness occurs.

Then I'll go alone to the curve of the lake
to see what will jump for me.

Estival

When the arms of the larkspur dial open
it's only natural to want to dissolve. In the glinting haze
you have nothing to do but keep moving

inward. Here's your realm of green sepals, tall
as knights. Your calyx sharpens over a dominion of seeds.
When the arms of the larkspur dial open

draw your wedding ring in mulch. Don't stand
around too long. Since all parts of the larkspur are toxic
you have nothing to do. Keep moving

with patience over the hooks & buttons of sun.
July is an alkaloid tongue, sunk in botanical Latin.
But when the arms of the larkspur dial open

you can learn to climb. All the way up
to the silent blue beak at the top of your thought.
There's nothing to do but keep moving

hand over hand. Time widens, just like your body
sealed shut in the light. An inner world hums
as the arms of the larkspur dial open.
There's nothing for you here. Move on.

Doubloon Oath

By dead gal or stove bones
by rainbow or red bird
red bird or cracked spine
by silk wrap or jaw jaw
by cold bodice, blush wing
tick tick or sunk ship
by tipped arrow, glass bite
by weird catch or *take that*
by chopped mountain, slick house
boatneck or gloss hog
striped awning, gold lawn
by *what's that* or *so much*
without me or full prof
full prof or nunchucks
blood orange, brain gob
time kill or toy star
by black doll or briar thorn
beg beg or gewgaw
by sweetmeat, or gunlock
or old maid or dreadnought
by weakness or whitecap
or grief-bacon, worksong
by fieldwork or field mix
slagged field or steel kilt
by bone-bruise or kneesock
I get my gift.

Three

I Married a Horseman

for his straight jaw & dark jackets.
For he gave me his ring to wear as a cinch.

My markings, he called *faint star*, *white boot*
& drew a line of rain

down the side of my cheek. I married him
for the silence in his speech, for

his black kerchief. All the time
he drew & in this drawing, we married.

Now I live in the timber scent & tall
smoke of his shadow. Evenings, he returns

to me from his work, with his fine coat
haltered in frost. This house

has no doors. We pass each other
crossing our necks in Hello.

Ghosts

After Anne Sexton

Some ghosts are my mothers
neither angry nor kind
their hair blooming from silk kerchiefs.
Not queens, but ghosts
who hum down the hall on their curved fins
sad as seahorses.

Not all ghosts are mothers.
I've counted them as I walk the beach.
Some are herons wearing the moonrise like lace.
Not lonely, but ghostly.
They stalk the low tidepools, flexing
their brassy beaks, their eyes.

But that isn't all.
Some of my ghosts are planets.
Not bright. Not young.
Spiraling deep in the dusk of my body
as saucers or moons
pleased with their belts of colored dust
& hailing no others.

Witch Wife

I'll conjure the perfect Easter
& we'll plant mini spruces in the yard—
my pink gloves & your green gloves

like parrots from an opera over the earth—
We'll chatter about our enemies' spectacular deaths.
I'll conjure the perfect Easter

dark pesto sauce sealed with lemon
long cords of fusilli to remind you of my hair
& my pink gloves. Your gloves are green

& transparent like the skin of Christ
when He returned, filmed over with moss roses—
I'll conjure as perfect an Easter:

provolone cut from the whole ball
woody herbs burning our tongues—it's a holiday
I conjure with my pink-and-green gloves

wrangling life from the dirt. It all turns out
as I'd hoped. The warlocks of winter are dead
& it's Easter. I dig up body after body after body
with my pink gloves, my green gloves.

Lament

I've lost something, an argument.
Even our rickshaw-wallah knows
& the women in jeweled sandals palming clear
lumps of jaggery. They do not squint
as we pass, but they can hear my buzz & bicker
pressed tight with you on this bench seat where dozens
of hot vinyl hearts brand the backs of my legs.
I think of the NyQuil I should've packed for us—
rainbow lake of sleep we could've sipped—
if I'd been a clever wife
if I'd heeded the cough & *achoo* of that guy
on the flight over from Newark.
I tell you *We got punished, this is punishment*
& I mean it with steam, as that father & son
rake yards of soaked cotton from their dye vats
sweat rolling down their noses, exact.
If I were sweeter, didn't boil with panic
I could've charmed the doctor into charging us less
for your X-rays & your ultrasound
for your glucose sticks & liver panels.
The second day of your fever, he complimented my arms
black with new henna & promised
you'd improve before they faded. He called
me *Madame* & I think I could've haggled.
Today there's no doubt about the itch

trailing its thin flag across my throat
or the translucent goo I honked into the sink
this morning. I've got what you've got, husband:
your white shirt, sweated through to the skin
your watery eyes & snow-cold hands. I do.

Vigil

You ask what I'm *not* a liar about. It's dark.
From bed, we watch some passing headlights rake
the windows back. I tell you how I see myself: alone
with my guitar, strappy heels, a bit of sweet pea
twisted through my hair. *But my fingers slide right off
the strings* I say, pulling up the covers. *They just
won't move at all.* By now, you've spun deep into the quilt.
Your arms are gone. *I'm telling you the truth* I say
about the guitar. I'm sitting up now. Almost, I can feel
the lacquered wood against my chest, a resonance
of thrumming spruce. You stir, then clock
the space between my hands. *There's nothing there*
you sigh. *Why make things up?* So I look again.
Left arm, right arm: crescented. There's something here
but not an instrument. It has some weight.
I notice how the quilt is tucked as if the cradled shape
could drift apart like antler velvet. I've never held
a form precise as that, in bundled cloth
nor felt its pulse go *zing* against my hand, & then—
my hands feel warm. More truly weighted than before.
I glimpse a momentary face, a tiny zero snugged within
my elbow's dark. I wrap the quilt. I keep
it close. All night, I try to count the hushed electrons
blooming in my brain. Whenever I dream of water
rippled leaves—the little face is sometimes there

& sometimes not, but here, or there, I almost say
I wish, then bite my lip to force it back. I sit up
like that for many nights, not knowing what I want
or don't. In Como, once, alone, I ate a fish I let
the waiter serve me with two spoons. I read Fitzgerald
twice. I loped in long brown boots & cried & made up
songs about myself. From the red funicular above the town
I watched the women hang their slips to dry. I watched them lift
their silver coffee pots & call their boys in from the street.
How neat I said, & memorized their clinking plates. I tracked
the twilight smack of soccer balls, the sound of thunder
making promises across the lake. *I'll write this down* I said
but that was all. I didn't want it more than anything. I didn't
think of *mom* or *bride*. I burned in my leather coat. I lied.

Prophecy

You have a good belly for twins. I can see you
at thirty weeks, your skin bright as automotive paint.
Rejoice, now: your life will be full of blessings.

Your twins wear little caps, little suits, on the bus.
They munch animal crackers under a striped shade.
See? You have a good belly for twins.

They'll remember you best in your pink gown.
Your hair cinnamon-dark, brushing your waist.
Rejoice, now: your life will be full of blessings.

Arrange raw almonds in a dish with lemon & salt.
This is how you'll be: whole, yielding. A planet.
You have a good belly for twins. I can see you

coming home to what you own. Your white
motorcar. Glass ornaments on the sills. Your twins
are such blessings. Rejoice, now, at your life

lined up like azaleas. Your life unfolding in air.
When will you take your turn at the spade?
I see you, twinned. But you have a good belly
for now. Rejoice in your blessings, you fool.

Confession

Every month I decide not to try
is a lungful of gold I can keep for myself.
Still, I worry you'll come to me anyhow

& hitch your hiccuping bud. My dear
I don't want to be got. I just want to get done
with this month. I decide not to try.

I decide on a wine. You keep spinning
through the woods on green stars of pollen.
Still, I worry you'll come to me anyhow.

Your small breath troubles the flour
I'm spilling. Did you leave sweet jam on the sill?
Every month, I decide not to try

to find out. Late sun butters the glitz
in my guts. My dear, I'm already botched.
Still, I worry you'll come to me anyhow.

Lately, I've dreamed of quilts stuffed
with bees; it's a thing. Yet I don't see
why I worry & worry. You come to me anyhow
every month I decide not to try.

The Child Was in the Woods

which woods pertained to glory. The Team
swept through, measuring the crinolines
of leaves. Humming in the woods, the child
slipped through blades of rain. Which rain
fell down in prayer again. The Team raised
shields against the acorn-glitz & swelling
bark. One knelt to track the beetle with its
carapace of sun. All this time, the child
was in the woods, her cells dividing
in medallions. She hummed & half her face
tangled in the trees, which trees were tongues
& yarns of fire. Still, the Team pressed on
through rows of violets crowned like crumbling
teeth, through glistered gaps the light licked
over. *Anywhere a buttercup could fit, this kid
could be* they hissed through slits of mics
that cracked & clung. The Team nodded

one by one. Even so, the child curled
deep in her rookery. There, she dreamed
of sitting in a painted room, a tiny chair
& table planted there. The child dreamed
of sitting in the tiny chair. She had to pluck
a harp with many strings. In her dream, she saw
two listeners: increments of ivory, bent
& silent at the door. *I won't be yours* the child

sang *No, not yours* then woke with a scorch
in her throat in the woods. Now the Team withdrew
their robes & instruments. They patted the dark
shells of the trees. *Sleep* they said. But the child
rose without pause, rose without pause
from her perch in the woods, from the brawny
tawny woods, which realm was deep
& oil-dark: was glory.

Prospera

I had a daughter like a trench plate once
she lidded my loneliness just so
that was before I retired to my Milan

where now I slide my tongue across
my own gapped teeth in the dark but
when I had my daughter, my trench plate

I poured water & stars, water & stars
she dreamed in the cradle I dug in the mud
& I didn't think of retiring to Milan

nor of losing my daughter to that dark
garnet of a husband & his talk
she was my trench plate daughter

& I hushed her to sleep all alone
in a language I drew from my own throat
but I've forgotten it here in Milan

where every third thought is my grave girl
waltzing in her wedding gown of wire
don't you miss how you were mine once, O
my trench plate, in another Milan

Four

Nursery

We opened the door to the fairy house
& took our tea on matching pebble seats.
Somehow we got out of there alive

though something crystalline of us
remains in that dark, growing its facets.
We opened the door to the fairy house

at the oak's black ankle. You asked
What could happen? as you disappeared
somehow. We got out of there alive

the strange tea still warm in our bellies.
Inside, our hosts gave damn few answers.
Who built that door? Is this a fairy house?

They had no faces yet. We spoke
into their quince-bud ears. You wept.
Somehow we got out of there alive

though we didn't quite return. Our life
is different now we've drunk the tea.
They're alive somehow. I got us out.
Why did you open the door to the fairy house?

Gräpple

Take the fond flesh of a *pomme* & haunt
it with food-grade chem: a grape soaking.
Nothing can go wrong with this plan.

Sometimes I worry my grandmama's ghost
glitched between passages. She pinches
too hard at my fond flesh, the haunted *pomme*

I am, when I know what I am I ain't enough
to make anyone linger. In the crisp, eerie light
nothing can go wrong with my plan

to stay here, on this side, & not call any spirit
into my bodily bruise, no starburst of cells
to haunt my fond flesh, round as a *pomme*.

Let my unhappy dead remain on their vines.
I'll bike beneath with my empty blood-basket.
Nothing can go wrong with this plan.

But it's hard to promise. Something still
considers me. Every night, I snarl myself
between a haunting & the fond flesh of a *pomme*.
It goes wrong. I start to plan.

Post-Apocalyptical

It happens at my desk: a gathering in. As if the room were a forehead graying at the lid. Even the light steps around & hovers just behind my eyes. I don't have to read & anyway the words march neatly off my screen, back to their nest in the wall or under the Coke machine where they can curl around each other until called. This is my job: to wait for the sweetie feeling inside me to swell to the size of a flapjack. I want to get hold of that same feeling inside another lifer. I mean the real sugar of it, roasted & packed like a warm thought. So I scrape my hair into a mess of woody stems. I chew & stare from my window over the roofs of the other world. Sometimes I see men in dark polo shirts pressing pistols to the bellies of passing choppers. Something happens but it doesn't keep happening. This is a careful time.

Ought

We'll have to hurry if we want to get started.
It's high time to consider beginning at all.
Time, at least, to think about starting

to start. After all, we've only just gotten up
& running, but now? We're almost too late.
We'll have to hurry. If we want to get started

we'll have to start now. We'll have to work
round the clock, round the clock, round the—
Well. Let's think about starting, at least. Though

it's tougher than ever. We can't even begin
to explain what it's like. To start with, we know
we should want to hurry. At least, we're starting

to want to. That's almost too tough to say
at the start. Still, we're sure we'll begin any moment.
It's time to get started we think. Let's consider

getting up & running. By then, it'll just sort of *start*
& we'll have begun. *Zut alors!* It's a plan & a party!
It's just—we *should* hurry. If we want to get started
we better begin. But it's tough. Just look at the time.

N/Ought

I must forgive myself for waiting so long.
I know a woman who waits is offensive
but I just can't get over my flaws

& now they might zero me out. My blood
is a zone of dispute, a tropic of fault. Since
I've waited so long, I must forgive myself.

Only—somehow I can't. My forgiveness snags
on my nexus of doubts. I know it's my fault
but there's no getting over the flaws

in my tropical blood, which may not carry on.
I don't know what I want. That's my offense.
But I must forgive myself for waiting so long

to decide. Does this prove I'm no good?
Because maybe I'm right on all counts . . . but
I just can't get over it all. My flaws

glister. My heart is a springhouse of doubt.
Don't blame me for not bellying up.
I've waited so long that I ought to forgive but
I just can't get over myself. It's a flaw!

Jantar Mantar

The king's instruments burn my hands when I touch them. The king's stairs burn my feet so I can't climb up or down. The land is pink, black, or pink-black. It sharpens in the sun. The sign above the king says: *Shimmy a path through my calculus.* When I look down, the path curves away into slices of egg. Each slice has a number painted black to honor the sun's penumbra & I'm crying as the slices vanish through a high arch. My stomach boils. Blood comes through my knee in gridded lines. Above me, dozens of pastel plinths romp in the yard. Some slide, huge as wedding cakes, some yawn like elephants over the white pellet of noon. The sun's penumbra has divorced the sun. I know it suddenly. That's why all colors have veins full of neon, why they must bleed to be seen. When I put my hand on a color, it feels animal-warm. I'm brushing the flank of a fine orange wall & tasting honey on my teeth when my life as the glass king begins.

The Temple at Govind Dev Ji

I'd like to go there once more
before I become a mother. I'd like to get
right up to the gates. Then, through—

I can believe at the absolute center.
Smoked air, running fountains.
I'd like to go there once more

& open my hands. Someone sings
at dawn in the sanctuary. I was there.
I walked right up to the gates. Then, through—

as though I deserved it. I took
off my shoes. I wore my garland
right up to the gates. Then, through—

where I held the wrists of a lady who smiled
& pronounced me *good*. Now I'm no mother
but I'd like to go there once more

& stand with the women. Saying the names
of belief. So many names I'd like to call out
once more, before I become another.
I'll go there once more, then, through—

Scarlet

Long ago, I was a *figlia* with a fever.
Little filly, foaled in my dark star-bed
where I thought I'd die pretty soon.

Lying there, my fists held candy eggs
of logic, molten math. My pink death already
long ago. I was a *figlia* with a fever

& I doubled in the neck. My neck?
Rather my baton, spilling white glitter.
Pretty. I thought I'd die soon

& warp to World 8-4. I'd take
a running jump up broken orange steps
to find my long-ago *figlia*. My fever

thinner than her thin dress falling
past her tender baby-knees. I knew her.
I thought I'd die pretty soon

& leave the shadow of my rash
hot patch of strawberry skin for her to keep
from long ago. Dearest *figlia*, my fever
was so soon. Thought I'd die pretty.

Letter to Monticello

I must apologize for leaving my seat in the middle of your summit on social justice. I hadn't meant to get up at all, but my headache finally forced me to twist past everyone else's drawn-up knees & folded tote bags, my mouth looping *Sorry, sorry*. Can I tell you about this headache? Gray & narrow, a fog helmet. I staggered down to your Farm Store to buy a small jug of chilled coffee & some extra-large peanuts, which I ate, slowly, on a bench. From there, I heard the keynote poet declare that we should send only black women astronauts to Mars. *You just know we'll make do with whatever we find up there* she said, her voice actually *dimpling* in a pleased way I'd never heard before. Your Farm Store caffeine entered my blood then, white stars dispersing. Did you know I gave up coffee last year? I turned thirty-six & thought *Maybe I should try for a baby*. Every month brought me closer to Mars, a planet ruled by black women astronauts. I can hardly talk about the headaches. Jefferson called peanuts *peendars*. He planted sixty-five hills of them in his garden once, or so it says on the back of the tin. I ended up not having a baby. But the peanuts! Quite tulip-shaped. Not like regular tulips, more like the old Turkish paintings where tulips first appear as chemical flames. I prefer them this way.

Purgatorio

I only want what I can't have
when my old terror stabs me in the neck.
The Lord teaches me to love without fear.

But I wake up in battledress, picking lice
off my collar. Hardtack. Heat lightning.
I only want what I can't have.

When will I get my great morning of wrath?
When my white deer self comes down from the woods?
The Lord teaches me to love without fear

but I drop my rifle & quickstep away
from all the dark between us. Tell me again how
I only want what I can't have?

Things must change. I must pray.
If rivers crested & forts collapsed, maybe then.
The Lord teaches me to love without fear.

When I dream of the future, I'm always alone.
Even now, something drags me with fear teeth.
I don't know what I want. I only love
what I'm Lord of. Teach me, or else.

Acknowledgments

I wish to thank the editors of the following journals and anthologies, where versions of these poems have appeared:

River Styx, "Self-Portrait"
Spoon River Poetry Review, "Young"
PEN Poetry Series, "New South" (as "Memoir"), "This is How We Feed the Animals," "Elegy"
jubilat, "Contagion"
The Spectacle, "First Girdle"
Wave Composition, "Little Gals"
Pangyrus, "Pastoral"
Memorious, "Nocturne," "Let Me Tell You People Something," "Why Don't You Wear a Black Crepe Glove Embroidered in Gold, Like the Hand That Bore a Falcon?"
Louisville Magazine, "Political Poem"
Tupelo Quarterly, "Afterlife"
Ploughshares blog, "Estival"
Los Angeles Review of Books, "Doubloon Oath"
Crazyhorse, "I Married a Horseman," "Lament"
Grimoire, "The Child Was in the Woods," "Witch Wife," "Prospera"
The Journal, "Vigil"
Green Linden, "Prophecy," "Confession"
Poetry, "Nursery"
Forklift, Ohio, "Sermon," "Twenty-One," "Gräpple"
Dusie, "Ought"

Prac Crit, "Scarlet"

Tarpaulin Sky, "Voice Lesson," "Purgatorio"

The poem "Thigh Gap" appeared in *Circe's Lament: Anthology of Wild Women Poetry*, edited by Bianca Lynne Spriggs and Katerina Stoykova-Klemer and published by Accents Publishing in 2016.

The poem "Doubloon Oath" appeared in *Best American Experimental Writing 2015*, edited by Seth Abramson, Jessie Damiani, and Douglas Kearney and published by Wesleyan University Press. Separately, it was produced in 2016 by Factory Hollow Press as a limited-edition chapbook, with illustrations by Philip Miller.

The poem "Jantar Mantar" was produced as a limited-edition broadside by Coconut Books in 2015.

The poem "Why Don't You Wear a Black Crepe Glove Embroidered in Gold, Like the Hand That Bore a Falcon?" takes its title from one of Diana Vreeland's "Why Don't You" columns in *Harper's Bazzar*.

"Political Poem" borrows lines from Martin Luther King Jr. and John Wilkes Booth.

I would like to thank the University of Louisville's Department of English and the College of Arts and Sciences, the International Writing Program at the University of Iowa, and the Hermitage Artist Retreat in Englewood, Florida, for their generous support of portions of this work. Christopher Merrill, Dan Rosenberg, Rebecca Myers, Kim Brooks, Kaethe Schwehn, Lauren Haldeman, Dina Hardy, Patricia Caswell, Bruce Rodgers, Sharyn Lonsdale, Sandi Hammonds, Alexis Orgera, Frank London, John Jahnke, Steve Kistulentz, Carmen Gimenez Smith, Rob Tarbell, Ruthie Stephens, Eve Beglarian, Daniel Levy, Chandrahas Choudhury, Anirudh Rathore, Mandvi Ranawat, and the staff of Hotel Dera Rawatsar in Jaipur, India, offered me friendship, hospitality, and inspiration during the writing process.

To my mother, Patricia, and my husband, Philip: stars & stars & stars.

Kiki Petrosino is the author of *Hymn for the Black Terrific* (2013) and *Fort Red Border* (2009), both from Sarabande Books. She holds graduate degrees from the University of Chicago and the University of Iowa Writer's Workshop. Her poems and essays have appeared in *Poetry, Best American Poetry,* the *New York Times, FENCE, Gulf Coast, Jubilat, Tin House* and online at *Ploughshares.* She is founder and coeditor of *Transom,* an independent online poetry journal. She is an Associate Professor of English at the University of Louisville, where she directs the Creative Writing Program. Her awards include a residency at the Hermitage Artist Retreat and research fellowships from the University of Louisville's Commonwealth Center for the Humanities and Society and the Virginia Foundation for the Humanities.

Sarabande Books is a nonprofit literary press located in Louisville, KY, and Brooklyn, NY. Founded in 1994 to champion poetry, short fiction, and essay, we are committed to creating lasting editions that honor exceptional writing. For more information, please visit sarabandebooks.org.